"I truly believe when you have finished reading this devotional, you will feel more refreshed, more equipped, and more fulfilled in your daily walk with God. In these pages you will find God-given insight in a deep, yet simplistic way. Jackie's view and understanding of God's word is powerfully led by truth and fact; always focusing on the heart of God. Every one of us go through our daily routine dealing with everyday situations and issues. This book will inspire and help bring clarity to your walk with Christ."

Daniel Eric Groves

Walking

a devotional
for life

Jackie Groves

Walking
  a devotional for life

ISBN# 0-9710450-4-6

Copyright © 2005 Jackie Groves

Published by:
        Daniel Eric Groves Ministries
        Jackie Groves
        P.O. Box 68
        Hudsonville, MI 49426

        www.danielericgroves.com

Photography by Kaley Kiewiet.
Cover design by Aaron Glenn.
Text design by Elsie Sommers.

Dedication

This devotional is dedicated to my wonderful husband, Daniel. Without your words of wisdom and encouragement, I would not be the woman that I am. You give me love and strength beyond what you are aware. My best gift was you and I am eternally grateful to God for blessing me so much with you. You lead me even when you aren't holding my hand. It was your encouragement that lead me to write this devotional, thus you share in the credit. Thank you, baby. I love you!

Introduction

Walking is something that we all do every day, in some shape or form. We all walk differently, though. Some of us walk tall and confident, while others of us walk uncertain and insecure. What makes each of us different? The answer is Christ inside of us. Whether or not we have Christ inside of us determines how we walk. At the same time, however, how closely we are following after Him determines what effect our walk will have.

As Christians, our light is supposed to shine so brightly that the people we encounter daily cannot help but be changed. The enemy knows God's plan, though, and he works very hard to trip us up in our walk — daily. There are so many different rocks and boulders we find along this path of life. How we handle them and how we let them mold us determines what effect we will have on this world.

The issues in this devotional are all very near and dear to my heart. I have experienced each and every one of them, as have many other Christians.

My heart is to encourage you and help you to see the light at the end of the tunnel. We experience many things in life. God often gives us revelation into those experiences so we may in turn help someone else. I pray this devotional blesses you and draws you closer into God's safety. Life will always give you road blocks — sometimes it may seem like the road has just been absolutely demolished — BUT God will always be waiting at the end. His arms are outstretched, waiting to help you over the rocky parts. There is one thing in life that will always be consistent and safe and that is our Heavenly Father. Walk, every day, in a way that brings glory to Him. Let the steps you take or don't take, be a reflection of how grateful you are for all He has done.

Why We Worship

"For you created my inmost being; you knit me together in my mother's womb. I praise you because I am fearfully and wonderfully made; your works are wonderful, I know that full well."
Psalm 139:13-14

Much too often we forget the real reason why we worship. There is one sole purpose behind worship, and that is to give our God all the honor that He deserves. Unfortunately, sometimes we get caught up in the act or the song and forget what the action of our praise symbolizes.

"For you created my inmost being; you knit me together in my mother's womb." We worship because there is no one in this entire creation that could ever love us like God. We worship because He first loved us, without justifiable reason. He loved us in spite of our sin and shame. We worship because nothing compares to the love that He has given us. We worship Him because He knows what is best for us and promises to always be there

for us and with us. We have one small act to grace Him with and that is our worship.

Beyond that, this one small act should become the motive for our very existence. We worship God with songs and by lifting our hands, but we are also supposed to worship God with our lives. Our every action should bring honor to God and be a good representation of our Maker. By living our lives in complete reverence to God and remembering with our every action why we were created, we are worshipping. There is no greater act of appreciation than this.

Faithful in the Small

"Whoever can be trusted with very little can also be trusted with much, and whoever is dishonest with very little will also be dishonest with much."
Luke 16:10

How many Christians do you know that say, "I want to do something really small for God"? Not too many, huh? Unfortunately, this leads to a common misconception. Society has made up a system of desirable and undesirable positions in life. The undesirables are often considered to be "small". The part that is misconceived, though, is the comparison between God's system and society's system. They are not even similar. There is no small duty for God's kingdom. The smallest act of faith is comparable to the greatest.

This is where God tests our hearts and our motives. He wants to see how serious we truly are about furthering His kingdom and honoring Him. If we are willing to minister in a tiny town with joy and thankfulness, then certainly we can be trusted with nations. The same is true in reverse. If we whine and groan and moan when we are asked to stand in the background without any recognition, then where is our heart? God will never move us on to the next season of life until we have learned the lesson He is trying to teach us in the present one. If God is going to trust us with thousands of His children, then He has to be certain that we can be trusted with one.

Always be thankful for whatever opportunity you are given. God will test you, so check your heart. Make sure you want to serve. Don't be afraid to do what the world would consider "menial" work. There are people whom you will encounter in those "menial" positions that are just as important to God as the glamorous people. Don't be afraid to be small. How faithful you are in the "small" determines how great the "big" will be.

The Presence of God

"But if we walk in the light of God's presence, as Jesus was in His light, we have fellowship with one another, and the blood of Jesus, purifies us from all sin." 1 John 1:7

The presence of God is where we find our power as Christians. If we choose to seek after God, we live in and are a part of the light that shines so brightly that everyone we encounter lives a little bit brighter because of God's presence in us. As we stay in God's will, He promises we will have fellowship with one another to keep us encouraged and lifted up. Yet, even more important than fellowship with each other, is the blood of Jesus. God's word says that Jesus' blood will purify us from all sin. There is nothing that won't be forgiven when we live in God's presence.

As Christians, we live in the world, but are not to be of the world, because we are supposed to be in the presence of God. In the presence of God, sickness cannot dwell, fear cannot entrap, and

Satan cannot touch us. In Psalm 16:1 David says to God, *"Keep me safe, O God, for in you I take refuge."* God's presence is our covering and our protection. Why would we step out into danger when we can have, for free, the safety of God's presence? Psalm 56:13 says, *"For you have delivered me from death and my feet from stumbling, that I may walk before God in the light of life."*

I want to encourage you to draw as close to God as you possibly can. Live in the presence of God daily. How do you do that? Spend time with Him all day long. Wherever you are and whatever you do, have God on your mind all day long. You can do that through music or reading or even just being around Godly people. God's presence should be evident in those that claim to be Christians. Your very existence will be an encouragement to others just because of the joy and confidence you walk in, knowing you live in God's light.

"You have made known to me the path of life; you will fill me with joy in your presence, with eternal pleasures at your right hand." Psalm 16:11

Learn to Preach

"The Spirit of the Sovereign Lord is on me, because the Lord has anointed me to preach good news to the poor." Isaiah 61:1

When someone mentions preaching, I know almost all of us think of preachers and pastors. Some of us think, "Oh, I'm not called to be a preacher. That scripture isn't about me." But the simple fact is that that scripture pertains to each and every one of us who profess to be a Christian.

There are three parts to this scripture that typically lead people to the above conclusion, and those are the words preach, good news, and poor. To *preach* in this scripture does not necessarily mean with words. A person's very actions can testify to the love of God, and many times few words are needed to be an example of love. We know the *good news* is the message of Christ. We often translate the word *poor* to mean financially poor. This scripture, however, is not speaking only of the poor in pocket, but especially of the poor in spirit, meaning those without a relationship with God. So now, with a better understanding of the word, we can see we are all called to be preachers in our sphere of influence. As children of God, it is our responsibility to never miss an opportunity to give someone the love of Christ — the best gift we can ever offer.

The first part of this scripture says that *"The Spirit of the Sovereign Lord is on me."* Thus, never be concerned that you are not equipped, because as a child of God, your best equipment is the Holy Spirit who lives inside you. So preach, preach with words, preach without, just preach.

Seeking Peace

"...Seek peace and pursue it." Psalm 34:14

This scripture is one my husband, Daniel, and I live by daily. We have learned that in all things and all decisions there is only one way to be lead, and that is by the peace of God. There is a difference, though, between comfort and peace. Comfort does not always indicate God's will. As a matter of fact, often it is a good sign that you might be getting a little lazy.

Comfort is when things or situations are not difficult at all, or the path that you have chosen does not have a stone in it. In other words, comfort is present when you have removed any opportunity to trust God to take care of you.

Peace, on the other hand, is entirely different. Peace is not always a comfortable situation. God's peace may lead you to make a decision that seems to be a bit risky when viewed through your human eyes. But the main difference between comfort and peace is this: with peace, you know God is holding your hand and leading you toward His blessings, no matter how difficult the choice it may be.

I want to encourage you to pray to God for peace. One of God's names is Jehovah-Shalom, which means the Lord our Peace. Pray that He will teach you discernment, so you can clearly know the difference between comfort and peace. Pray you will know His plans by His peace.

"I have told you these things, so that in me you may have peace. In this world you will have trouble. But take heart! I have overcome the world." John 16:33

I Am Love

"Love is patient, love is kind. It does not envy, it does not boast, it is not proud. It is not rude, it is not self-seeking, it is not easily angered, it keeps no record of wrongs. Love does not delight in evil but rejoices with the truth. It always protects, always trusts, always hopes, always perseveres. Love never fails." 1 Corinthians 13:4-8

My encouragement for you today revolves solely around this one message. It is one of the greatest messages in the Bible. To begin with, I want you to think about what or who has been the greatest representation of love in the history of the world. Do you have your answer? Well, the correct answer is Jesus. He paid the most sacrificial price for you and me, purely because of His love for us. The Bible says we have the power to do what Jesus did and we are called to be like Him. Thus, our lives are to be a representation of Christ — pure love.

My challenge for you is to speak this scripture over yourself each and every day. Confess with your mouth that you are love and all of its attributes. Believe in your heart that you are loving and kind, and watch your countenance and character change.

*"I am patient, I am kind. I do not envy, I do not boast, I am not proud. I am not rude, I am not self-seeking, I am not easily angered, I keep no record of wrongs. I do not delight in evil but rejoice with the truth. I always protect, always trust, always hope, always persevere. **I never fail.**"*

Pleasing God vs Pleasing Men

"Am I now trying to win the approval of men, or of God? Or am I trying to please men? If I were still trying to please men, I would not be a servant of Christ." Galatians 1:10

Sometimes we make it hard to be a Christian. We want the best of both worlds. We want to be the best Christian there is. At the same time, we want to be the most popular person — loved by everyone. Somehow we just can't have both. We simply can't please both God and men all the time.

As hard as it is to forget about those silly things in life we want, they aren't nearly as important as our eternal life with God. This earth will pass away, but our relationship with God is forever. Choosing to be a Christian is essentially choosing to forget about pleasing anyone except God. Paul said in Galatians that if he were still trying to please men, he would not be a Christian because that is not the reason for this life.

It is, however, what Satan wants to make us think life's about. He throws concerns around about what people think of us or if we are accepted, but we know where our identification lies. We know what God thinks of us — great, loving, adoring thoughts. Plus, we are certain we are more than accepted. He sent His only Son to die a tremendous, horrific death because He wants nothing more than to be with us for eternity.

Often we don't even notice how easily we can be distracted by our tendencies to want to please man, but we have to be intentional. We have to intentionally choose, everyday, who we are going to serve. We have to wake up every morning and commit the day to God so no other thoughts or agendas can get in the way. There is no greater joy in life than to be found pleasing in the Lord's sight. Seek Him first, before anything or anyone else, and there will most certainly be years and years of joy to come.

"May the words of my mouth and the meditation of my heart be pleasing in your sight, O Lord, my Rock and my Redeemer." Psalm 19:14

Untouchable

"A thousand may fall at your side, ten thousand at your right hand, but it will not come near you." Psalm 91:7

When you live your life for Christ, you live under His covering. No harm can come upon you. If you are an effective Christian, meaning one that is leading others to Christ and seeking after God, then Satan's primary goal is to wipe you out. He would love nothing more than to just remove you from the earth, so that he doesn't have to lose any more souls to God. Here is the question that you should ask yourself, "Do I really believe that Satan has the power to harm a hair on my head?" Here is your answer, "No!"

Satan does not have the power to harm you. The only way for Satan to be empowered would be if you were to step away from God. If you allow yourself to be outside of God's covering and His protection, then yes, you are more susceptible to Satan's attacks. Satan only has what power you give him. God left your life up to you. He gave you all the tools to be prosperous and blessed, but He gave you the choice. You can either trust Him with your life or throw the power Satan's way by trusting yourself.

In God there is eternal protection and safety. He is a protective Father that has His eyes on His children at all times. He will never let anyone step in to harm you. Isaiah 41:11 says, *"All who rage against you will surely be ashamed and disgraced; those who oppose you will be as nothing and perish."* Next time you feel threatened or attacked, just remember your protection may not be seen with your eyes, but it is greater than all of creation.

"So do not fear, for I am with you..." Isaiah 41:10

"We are hard pressed on every side, but not crushed; perplexed, but not in despair; persecuted, but not abandoned; struck down, but not destroyed." 2 Corinthians 4:8-9

Avoid Whom?

"But now I am writing you that you must not associate with anyone who calls himself a brother but is sexually immoral or greedy, an idolater or a slanderer, a drunkard or a swindler. With such a man do not even eat." 1 Corinthians 5:11

The topic of which people to associate with is one that has been debated for years. Like everything else, though, the answer is in the Bible. 1 Corinthians 5:11 says not to associate with the "brother", meaning brother in Christ, who is sexually immoral or greedy, etc. This scripture tells us not to associate with believers that fall into these categories.

Unfortunately, this scripture is typically taken out of context. If we look back to 1 Corinthians 5:10, we see that it says, "not at all meaning the people of this world who are immoral, or the greedy and swindlers, or idolaters." Thus, the Bible specifically says not to associate with those who claim to be Christians, but live just like the world.

As much as we don't like the phrase "guilty by association", it's absolutely true. If we spend our time with hypocritical Christians we may be thrown into that category and there goes any influence we might otherwise have had. Instead, we should not be afraid to have a good influence on those who need to be influenced.

If you have the strength of character to be set apart from the world, then don't be afraid to touch them. If your faith is enough to keep you from being tempted, then your job is to reach out to those that need Jesus, no matter what their worldly reputation.

"But the one who does not know and does things deserving punishment will be beaten with few blows. From everyone who has been given much, much will be demanded; and from the one who has been entrusted with much, much more will be asked." Luke 12:48

Send Me

"Then I heard the voice of the Lord saying,
'Whom shall I send? And who will go for us?'
And I said, 'Here am I. Send me!'" Isaiah 6:8

Isaiah's heart was willing. How many of us trust enough to just say, "God, send me wherever"? A heart like Isaiah's is all God is waiting for. He has proven Himself time and time again, yet we still don't put our entire trust in Him. I know that some of us think, "But if I tell Him that, He could send me to Africa." That very thought is fear. It is fear of a number of things: fear that you will fail; fear that you will be alone; and fear that you aren't strong enough for such a "big" mission. But see, every mission in your Christian life is a big one, because lives hang in the balance.

The greatest honor in my life is knowing that every day God wants to use me to impact someone else's life. I am so flattered that my God, who knows all, trusts me with another one of His children. Just His confidence in me helps me to realize that there is nothing I can't do through His strength.

If God would trust you enough to send you, don't you think you should just consider the idea that you are equipped to go? The Bible says you are. The whole point behind being a Christian is leading other people to the same salvation you have in Christ. If you live in fear and think you are not capable of doing that, you are right where Satan wants you — a Christian convinced you are powerless, and therefore essentially useless to God's kingdom. But God says we are all more than conquerors through Christ.

Matthew 22:14 says, *"For many are invited, but few are chosen."* I believe few are chosen, because many do not believe in the power of God within them, so they will not step up and say, "God, here I am, send me." God created you to do great things for His kingdom. The God that can see all and knows all, knows exactly what He put inside you. Trust that He will never leave your side and never give you a load greater than you can bear. Step up, trust Him, and just go. He is waiting for you to surrender your fear and your will and to take on His power.

When You Believe

"If you believe, you will receive whatever you ask for in prayer." Matthew 21:22

The possibilities are endless when you believe. I am not talking about just hoping for something, I mean expecting, just like you expect your next breath. Believing in God, and believing in whatever you ask of Him, is the same thing as trusting Him. You cannot receive your salvation without believing. Romans 10:9 says, *"That if you confess with your mouth, 'Jesus is Lord,' and believe in your heart that God raised him from the dead, you will be saved."* The very first step that you take as a new Christian has to be taken with belief in your heart. Every step that you take from then on has to be followed with the same expectation.

In Luke, the woman with the bleeding disease knew if she just touched the edge of Jesus' cloak, she would be healed. She expected that if she could just touch Him, some of His power would leave Him and she would have to be healed. Jesus noticed her and said, *"Daughter, your faith has healed you. Go in peace."*

Right after that, a man named Jairus, wanted Jesus to heal his sick daughter. When Jesus heard of this, he told him, *"Don't be afraid; just believe, and she will be healed."*

There is nothing you cannot have if you just believe. Don't allow your thoughts to set a boundary on what God is capable of doing. You know He is able to do more than you can imagine. Expect miracles and watch them unfold.

God's Plans vs Our Plans

"'For I know the plans I have for you,' declares the Lord, 'plans to prosper you and not to harm you, plans to give you hope and a future.'"
Jeremiah 29:11

Most of us, as children, decide what we want to be when we grow up. Some of us teeter back and forth between a few things, and some of us pick just one and work toward that goal. Sometimes those goals are from God and sometimes we just get an idea in our heads and run with it. We can plan our whole lives out before we know it, and never once have checked with God.

I know I had my whole life figured out. I had my college totally planned, and then had made plans for grad school. I had even planned out my career, and when my husband would come along to marry me. I had even gone so far as to decide when Mystery Husband and I would have children. Then, when nothing went according to plan I finally realized that God must have just been laughing at me from up there. I was taking my life into my own hands and not leaving anything up to God. Proverbs 19:21 says, *"Many are the plans in a man's heart, but it is the Lord's purpose that prevails."*

Always invite God to be a part of the everyday portions of your life — the planning stages. One thing you cannot do in life is succeed without working from God's map. Even when you aren't intentionally trying to figure it out on your own, if you haven't sought after God for your answers, then you are relying on yourself and probably your own strength. God is the only one with all the answers. Let Him plan your course and you definitely won't get lost.

"But seek first his kingdom and his righteousness, and all these things will be given to you as well."
Matthew 6:33

Learning to Be Still

"I will fight for you, you need only to be still."
Exodus 14:14

One of the hardest things for us, as people and as Christians, is being still. We often convince ourselves that our productivity and/or busyness determines our value. This is one of those little lies that Satan whispers to many of us.

Another reason most people do not like to be still is that it leaves us vulnerable and open for people to see what we are made of. Today's society has convinced us that we cannot trust. Unfortunately, this trust issue runs over into God, as well.

God does not have the capability to leave us or forsake us. He says in His word that He will fight for us; that we just need to be still. How simple it sounds, yet how difficult we make it. He has made His word simple enough even for a child to understand. God has called each and every one of us to have a child-like faith. What is the difference between a child and an adult? A child has not yet been affected by the world, thus their level of trust is much greater. A child will take God's words for their simplicity and not over-analyze them as adults tend to do. God has commanded only that we be still and let Him fight for us — let Him take care of our battles. In doing so, we must trust that when we stand still, He has us protected on every side and no harm can reach us.

Setting a Standard

"Live such good lives among the pagans that, though they accuse you of doing wrong, they may see your good deeds and glorify God on the day he visits us." 1 Peter 2:12

Our main goal in life, as Christians, is to lead people to Christ. In doing so, there are obviously many worldly things we have to avoid. The Bible says that we live in this world, but we are not of this world. One of the largest stumbling blocks to non-believers, in my opinion, is inconsistency amongst believers. We are supposed to be living our lives above reproach and setting an example, but so often it is hard to differentiate a person who professes to be a Christian from someone who does not.

As Christians, we have to set the standard. We have to determine, based on Godly principals, what is a good representation of Christ and what is not. Much too often Christians do not avoid the gray areas like they should. For instance, the topic of alcohol is one that many Christians will dance around. Is alcohol evil in itself? No. Did Jesus even drink wine? Yes. Now answer this question. How does today's society, as a whole, perceive it? Society overall, perceives alcohol as an ungodly thing. In most situations, if a pastor were seen having a beer in a restaurant, it would be tainting to his/her reputation. Thus, the conclusion to be drawn is to steer clear.

As Christians, we need to always consider our witness. If something we do or do not do could cause someone to stumble or question God, then we should not even think twice about doing it again. Philippians 1:27 says, *"Whatever happens, conduct yourselves in a manner worthy of the gospel of Christ."*

No matter where you are and no matter who is or isn't watching, someone will see. That someone could be God or that someone could be a non-believer. Set a standard with your life that can never be questioned.

Unchanging Father

"I the Lord do not change..." Malachi 3:6

People, sometimes, can be really hard to figure out. It seems like as soon as you figure them out, they change something. This makes it kind of hard to get to know them, much less start to trust them. If a person isn't consistent it's harder to feel safe in a relationship with them. That is why our relationship with God is so secure. God isn't man, nor does He change. The Lord promises that He will not change. He didn't say, "If you don't make me mad, I'll be consistent", or "If you never mess up, I won't change." There are no exceptions. He just doesn't change.

Since we know that God doesn't change, we can breathe a little easier. We can always count on Him to love us, no matter what. We can always count on Him to fight for us, no matter what. We can always count on Him to never leave us. There is no greater promise than the promise of eternal love.

I want to encourage you to really think about what that promise means. Compare the idea to a person whom you love and trust more than anything. Has that person ever hurt your feelings? Have they ever disappointed you, even if it was unintentional? Now I want you to think about God. How much more trustworthy and loving is He? Never lose sight of the fact that the love of the Father is the only unchanging love there ever was, is now, or ever will be. Always place it before all else and watch His unfailing love be the greatest comfort you will ever know.

Fear

"There is no fear in love, but perfect love drives out fear." 1 John 4:18

Fear is another issue I have dealt with quite a bit in my life. Fear is like many of the other lies that Satan tells us; it starts as a little scare and then builds into torture. The more fear comes in and takes over, the less room there is for faith.

As we begin to hold on to fear in an area of our lives, we are essentially saying to God, "God, I can't trust you to take care of me in this area." We don't intentionally say that to God, but that is what our actions are saying. Jesse Duplantis says that "fear tolerated is faith contaminated." When we allow Satan to grip us so much with fear, we are taking the power back from God and giving Satan the control to determine what we will or will not do.

Your fear can only harm you, but trusting God can only bless you. Psalm 34:4 says, *"I sought the Lord, and he answered me; he delivered me from all my fears."* Fear is psychological most of the time. Just like Satan convinced you to fear, let God remind you of His protection. God will never let any harm come to you, but your faith must be in Him. Remind yourself that God cares as much for you as any other person in this world. Hold onto His promises and tell Satan he has no power. The more you trust in God, the less you will remember the fear. You can choose either fear or faith. The choice is simple, but it will determine how effective you are as a believer.

"So do not fear, for I am with you; do not be dismayed, for I am your God. I will strengthen you and help you; I will uphold you with my righteous hand." Isaiah 41:10

What Does the Lord Require?

"...And what does the Lord require of you? To act justly and to love mercy and to walk humbly with your God." Micah 6:8

I believe that much of the time, we Christians can be overwhelmed by this very question. And I believe a large part of that overwhelmed feeling comes from Satan. Satan tries to convince us that God is a dictator — that He sits on His throne barking out commands and orders, just waiting for us to trip and fall so He can say, "You messed up. Oh well, eternal condemnation for you!" But that is not God's character. God is a loving Father who watches His children make mistake after mistake, but is always right there with His hand out-stretched, waiting to pull us back into His safety.

The book of Micah says that God requires only three things of us. How simple He makes it, but once again, we confuse it with our lack of under-standing. God asks us to *act justly*. Something that is *just* is fair and impartial in action or judgment.

In other words, we must leave the judgment of others to God, and be forgiving and kind; willing to lend a hand when it is not deserved. Webster goes as far as to say "morally right". We, as Christians, are familiar with the meaning of the term "morals".

Secondly, God says to *love mercy*. Mercy can be described as kind treatment. God says to love it; to love to bless others by your actions and patience with them, regardless of the scenario. Give mercy where mercy isn't due.

Last, He asks that we *walk humbly with Him*. To walk humbly with Him means seeking after His will and choosing His path for our lives, while at the same time remembering that this life is not about us. There is much greater purpose in living than fulfilling ourselves. We have one main goal in life, and that is to see our Father fulfilled and to find His favor.

Though perfection may be what you *thought* God asked of you, it certainly is not. He doesn't expect perfection. Matter of fact, in the Bible He chose to use the broken pot. God only requires three simple things. You can either choose to simply follow after Him, or make it rough by adding clutter. I pray you will choose to simplify.

Prayer

"...You do not have, because you do not ask God."
James 4:2

"...The prayer of a righteous man is powerful and
effective." James 5:16

I had a great revelation on prayer a year or so ago. When an unfortunate or upsetting situation arose, I found I would think to myself, "Well, I guess there isn't really anything that I can do to help. I guess I'll just pray," as if prayer was a last resort. I became convicted when I realized that I was pushing God's intervention way back to last place, and even then not having much confidence that He would fix the situation.

Sometimes we forget that our prayers do mean something. Sometimes we are just so caught up in what we are doing that we forget to pray, which the Bible says is why we don't have what we want. Our prayers are the catalysts of change in this life and we must not forget that fact.

I know that because our faith is such a way of life, we often forget just how much power is behind our requests to God. Proverbs 15:8 says, *"...God delights in the prayer of the upright."* He loves it when we ask Him for things. Remember as you encounter life, that God is waiting for your requests. Nothing you can ask of God is too great or too small. If He knows the number of hairs on your head, surely He cares about the concerns of your heart.

"The Lord will perfect that which concerns me."
Psalm 138:8

Don't Lose Heart

"Therefore, since through God's mercy we have
this ministry, we do not lose heart."
2 Corinthians 4:1

It's very easy to get frustrated when the ministry God has led us to isn't perfect. Perfection is a subconscious expectation. We just always expect that the place we are heading toward will be better than the place we left. But generally, God moves us on to a bigger challenge. If there was already perfection in our ministries, then why would God need us?

The simple truth is that God will usually lead us to a place where we can have a positive influence in order to help bring about a change. However, God never promised it would be easy. Whenever we are doing work for the kingdom of God, we will always face opposition. That is Satan's job. We shouldn't be surprised when we encounter attacks; instead we should just be prepared.

Losing heart is not even an option. When we sit back and really think about the process, we realize how encouraging it is. To know that God trusts us to take care of some of His children is enough to fill us with confidence. Plus, Satan doesn't attack those Christians that aren't accomplishing things. He is only intimidated when we are helping people look to God.

So the next time you face adversity, count it all joy, because it means you are heading in the direction God intended. You have the power to change your scenario. Don't lose heart, but rather be filled with the power of God, and watch Him move your mountain.

You'll Never Be Alone

"No one will be able to stand up against you all the days of your life. As I was with Moses, so I will be with you; **I will never leave you nor forsake you.**" *Joshua 1:5*

This is one of my absolute favorite scriptures in the Bible. This promise makes me feel safe, as it should. During my childhood, my experiences formed a fear of abandonment within me. I grew up fearing that the people I loved would leave me. And then I found my comfort in my Heavenly Father who promised me that He would *never* leave me.

I know what I felt during most of my adolescent years and into my young adult life is a fairly common fear, and one with which the enemy plagues many Christians. I had to come to a place where I realized that my Heavenly Father was the most important thing in life and that He loved me beyond my wildest dreams. When I truly grasped the idea that He was always there and that I was never alone, I developed a Godly confidence. My faith grew so much that I knew there was nothing I couldn't accomplish because God would always be on my side.

God promises you, just as He promises me, that He will never leave you nor forsake you. That means the Creator of the world is right by your side, in good times and bad. He will defend you until the end of the earth. If ever you feel alone — don't. Remind yourself of God's promise and how safe it is in His arms.

Power of the Tongue

"The tongue has the power of life and death..."
Proverbs 18:21

"He who guards his lips guards his life, but he who speaks rashly will come to ruin."
Proverbs 13:3

There are a number of scriptures in the Bible that talk about how powerful the tongue is. So often we take for granted that our tongues have the power over life and death. We can either choose to speak life or we can choose to speak death. Our words can either be curses or blessings.

If we would learn to take our thoughts captive, then we would be better able to control our tongues. Once we grasp how powerful the tongue is, we have no excuse but to make a change. As Christians, our faith should always lead us to speak out our optimistic thoughts.

Our days are numbered by the words of our mouths. 1 Peter 3:10 says, *"Whoever would love life and see good days must keep his tongue from evil and his lips from deceitful speech."* Thus, we must be a people who understand the power of our tongues. We must be the ones who are eternally optimistic because we know the truth, and because we know that whatever we speak, we will have. God knows that our world needs some hope. Let us be the carriers of such encouragement by our words.

God Makes No Mistakes

"You will be secure, because there is hope; you will look about you and take your rest in safety."
Job 11:18

So many people, of every gender and race, face insecurities. All of us, myself included, at one point or another, have criticized ourselves because we weren't perfect enough. In our self-criticism, we truly believe we aren't happy with ourselves. However, many times our shame really comes from thinking others are not happy with us. The ironic thing for Christians, though, is that we allow Satan to make us feel inferior about something that is fading. The majority of self-doubt is caused by dissatisfaction with our physical bodies. We very rarely ever beat ourselves up over the state of our heart, which is much more important. Instead, we find fault with our flesh, even though it is not the portion of us that lasts forever.

There are so many things wrong with buying into Satan's lie. First, we are actually questioning whether or not God made a mistake in creating us.

By wishing we could have a different nose, or hairline, we are wishing we could go back and redo what God chose for us. Does that sound a little silly? In Psalm 139:13, it says, *"For you created my inmost being; you knit me together in my mother's womb."* If we believe He created us, then why don't we believe He made us as He saw best?

Secondly, if Satan can keep us focused on 'me, me, me', we won't see the bigger picture. When our eyes are only focused on what is going on with us, we miss the opportunities God puts before us every day. Matthew 6:21 says, *"For where your treasure is, there your heart will be also."* If our main focus in life is our exterior or our 'imperfections', then there is our treasure and Satan has succeeded in disabling us.

The only opinion in this life that matters is God's. Throughout your life, many people will speak over you. Learn to have selective ears. Only allow your heart to receive the words that are from the Lord, directly or indirectly. You were created for so much, but you must see past yourself to do it. Never let something that God created for good, be used to cause you harm. In God's eyes, you are absolutely the most beautiful person! If He doesn't see any flaws, then neither should you.

Seeing Past Pain

*"Cast your cares on the Lord and he will sustain
you; he will never let the righteous fall."*
Psalm 55:22

In my life, I have experienced some painful situations. I know when we experience loss and/or hurt in life we tend to wonder where God was and why He allowed and/or still allows painful things to occur. I know this is a painful topic in itself, but I also know we serve a gracious and merciful God.

The Bible says that He will never give us a load greater than we can bear. I believe, though, that the only way we can bear anything is through His strength. Therefore, to be able to sustain the load we are given, we must entirely rely on Him to pull us through. I know God never intends for us to go through pain — ever — but I also know that He will enable us to grow in the midst of the worst circumstances, if we so choose.

When we encounter pain and hurt, we have one of two choices. We can either choose faith and allow the situation to help us believe and trust in God even more, or we can choose to fear. In fearing, we aren't trusting God, nor are we believing His word. We are not all-knowing — that is God. We can't possibly comprehend the why's and how's of most situations.

We also need to remember we live in a fallen world and God has given us a choice. We determine the paths our lives will take, and either we give God the reins or we try to steer all by ourselves. Sometimes we don't understand why things happen, but we can cling to God's word, which is the only truth in this world. Psalm 23:6 says, "*Your love and mercy will follow after me all the days of my life.*" Believe in His word, and trust Him to sustain you.

Take a Stand

*"Speak up for those who cannot speak for them-
selves, for the rights of all who are destitute."*
Proverbs 31:8

As I have mentioned numerous times, our lives
are to be an example. We live in a world that is
void of compassion and mercy. Again, we are to
live in this world, but we are not to be of this
world. We are to be different.

God expects us to love and live as Jesus did. He
gave us all the same power. Jesus never walked
past a person in need without doing something.
Our eyes and our hearts should be open to those
less fortunate than we are. It is very easy to turn
our heads. Many Christians feel so overwhelmed
by the needs in the world that they begin to feel
that their contribution would not even make a difference. How quickly we forget that Jesus lives
inside of us.

I want to encourage you to take note of the need in your community. There is always something more that we, as followers of Christ, can do. Take a stand in defending those who are unable to defend themselves. Pray that God will fill you with compassion and a desire to make a difference. If you reach one person and show them the love of Christ, you have effectively changed your community. Change begins with one, whether that is changing your mind, your opinion, or your world. In the end, you will stand before God and He will want to know what you did with what you were given. Remember the faces and hands of each person you touch, so on that day, you can stand before God, humbly, and tell Him you loved His children.

Temptation

"No temptation has seized you except what is common to man. And God is faithful; he will not let you be tempted beyond what you can bear. But when you are tempted, he will also provide a way out so that you can stand under it."
1 Corinthians 10:13

Let's just face it: at one point or another, we have all been tempted. It just happens. Satan did it to Adam and Eve and he tries it with you and me just the same. Being tempted is an every day occurrence. We know temptation will come, but what is more important is how we respond to it and what happens after it has gone.

Temptation is temptation, whether it is indulgences, fleshly, etc, they are all the same. Does the temptation make someone a sinner? Absolutely not; even Jesus was tempted. When an opportunity for temptation arises, God's grace is present to overcome, no matter what the scenario. Ecclesiastes 1:9 says, *"...there is nothing new under the sun."* No temptation the enemy can throw at you takes God by surprise. He is right there waiting for you to pick up His strength and laugh in the devil's face.

Whenever temptation does try to cause you to stumble, I encourage you to remember that God is faithful, and that He won't let you be tempted beyond what you can bear. Every time you deny Satan when he comes with a temptation, you are one step closer to wearing him down. Don't give him any other option but his own defeat.

Rest

"Come to me, all you who are weary and burdened, and I will give you rest. Take my yoke upon you and learn from me, for I am gentle and humble in heart, and you will find rest for your souls. For my yoke is easy and my burden is light." Matthew 11:28-30

Life can be incredibly overwhelming at times. The mundane tasks of everyday life can sometimes clutter our minds and cause us to break down. As life gets busy — and it always will — you must always take the time to be still and rest in God's arms. There is nothing more fulfilling than resting for a moment and breathing a breath of the life with which God has blessed you.

Our tendency as humans is to focus on the not-so-positive aspects of life. When you find yourself there, remember to think of how easy God's yoke is and how light is His burden. When life seems to have you cornered, remember that God promises if we just say, "God, can you please take this burden from me? I am absolutely worn down," He will come in and rescue us. When a burden is lifted by God it is like a whole new beginning. And that is exactly as God intended. He wants you to be able to rest in Him and trust Him to take care of whatever it is that weighs you down.

What is Faith?

"Now faith is being sure of what we hope for and certain of what we do not see." Hebrews 11:1

Faith is a hard topic for many people, saved and unsaved, to grasp. The idea of believing in someone whom we cannot see is a bit far-fetched to some. Even for those who do believe, faith is a hard quality to maintain at all times.

Faith is a state of mind, or a decision. Faith is the knowing of God's mercies before having the need to exercise them. Our faith leads us to the confidence that God's word is true and our faith tells us to trust Him in all situations.

"Faith is being sure of what we hope for and certain of what we do not see." In other words, we cannot rely on our human eyes to tell us the truth. God tells us the truth, whether through audible words, or confirmations and circumstances. Pastor Duane Vander Klok says, "We see through our eyes, but we see with our heart." Our eyes are still

a part of our flesh, but our heart belongs to our spirit man, and will not lead us down a fleshly road.

Our faith must never be shaken by what happens on this earth. We know the only truth there is: the love of our Heavenly Father. Our faith tells us not to receive a bad report, because God is in control and blesses us with good things. Therefore, our faith is what we know in our hearts. Our faith should determine our actions. Either we can step out in faith, or shrink back in fear. Choose faith — it is the only road that leads to life.

God's Perfect Strength

"But he said to me, 'My grace is sufficient for you, for my power is made perfect in weakness.'"
2 Corinthians 12:9

I absolutely love this scripture. I have found so much comfort in knowing that I don't have to always be strong. I grew up thinking I did. I grew up thinking that to be weak was one of the worst qualities an individual could have. But one day, I found out that I was as weak as weak gets. I realized that when I work alone, without God's help, all I have is weakness and incapability. Eventually I learned I am everything that is weak, but God inside me is absolute strength.

When you trust in God your true strength shows through. David didn't defeat Goliath because of his strength. He defeated Goliath because he trusted that even though he was weak compared to Goliath, God would be his strength. There will always be things in life that can somewhat break you, but those are the times to remember that Jesus was broken so you would never have to be weak again. In and of yourself, you have no real strength, only false confidence and pride. But when you say, "God, I can't do this without you, please help me," God's perfect strength rises up inside you.

Hard times and disappointments sometimes convince you that you have to be strong, but that is not always true. In those times, remember to be weak before God, for in that weakness, God's strength will save you. When you realize you can't do anything without God and your strength is not enough, God's strength is made perfect in you. There is nothing that God's perfect strength cannot overcome.

Throwing Stones

"Why do you look at the speck of sawdust in your brother's eye and pay no attention to the plank in your own eye?" Matthew 7:3

This is a lesson nearly all mothers have tried to teach their children at one time or another: "If you can't say something nice, don't say anything at all." Why don't we listen? We know better than to be judgmental and hateful, so why are we?

The problem is that cynicism and criticism sneak in when we aren't paying attention. It starts with a small "harmless" comment and then it festers and grows into a huge mound of yuck in our hearts. The words we speak about other people aren't harmless by any means. Every word we say has power to either be positive or negative. When we speak something negative about someone, we are essentially speaking curses over them.

The second part of this problem is the one that carries the most irony. We always notice everyone else's flaws when we ourselves are filled with them. Most of the time, we just don't want anyone else to notice our problems, so we ridicule others, hoping to remove the attention from us.

Judging people and showing contempt for them displeases God greatly. Remember the woman caught in the act of adultery that was brought to Jesus? The best part of the story was Jesus' response. He said, *"If any one of you is without sin, let him be the first to throw a stone at her."* We all should remember this every time we pick up the "stone" of a critical thought or attitude. Remember what price was paid so we all may be forgiven.

Power of Your Confession

"Reckless words pierce like a sword, but the tongue of the wise brings healing." Proverbs 12:18

The power behind your confession is your faith. As Christians, we should live by our faith even when our physical bodies do not feel it. Our physical bodies are just that — physical — flesh and bone. Our faith is based on our spirit, thus we must tell our bodies to line up with the word of God. We already know our tongues have power over life and death, so they also have the power over our healing. The tongue of the wise brings healing, and we, as Christians, are the wise. In order for our tongues to bring healing we have to speak it out.

Just as our faith is hoping in what is not seen, so is our confession. Luke 18:42 says, *"Jesus said to him, 'Receive your sight; your faith has healed you.'"* When a person's physical body is not lining up with the word of God, we must speak the word of God over that person. Pastor Duane Vander

Klok says, "Don't talk *about* your mountain, but rather talk *to* your mountain." Along the same lines, Kenneth Copeland says,"Things will begin turning around for good in your life if you will cease speaking to God about the size of your problem and begin speaking to your problem about the size of your God."

When you or someone near you is being attacked by sickness, it is your job; since you are filled with Christ; to believe and speak forth positive words of encouragement. As a Christian, you can speak to that sickness and tell it to leave. Your faith is no faith at all without actions. Let your confession speak for your faith.

Why Worry?

"Who of you, by worrying, can add a single hour to his life?" Matthew 6:27

I know that I, personally, used to worry, worry, worry. Everything I did, I wondered if I had done it right, or if someone would think something ill of me. I would worry whether I got the job; whether I was a good enough Christian. When Daniel and I were dating, I used to worry about how much he loved me. You name it, I worried about it, and I know I wasn't alone. I have spoken with so many who worry constantly. I didn't realize what worry really was until I got some revelation from my wise husband. Worry is fear, plain and simple. There is no lighter or easier way to put it: they are one in the same.

Have you ever thought about what you are saying to God when you worry about things? You are simply conveying to God that you don't completely trust Him to take care of you. That is what your worry is. You worry because you aren't convinced that God truly has your best interests at heart. God said in Jeremiah 32:27, *"I am the Lord, the God of all mankind. Is anything too hard for me?"* What do you think? Do you think that there is anything too hard for God? Your worry says you think there are some things God can't or won't take care of for you. I want to encourage you to remember that thought the next time you try to handle your situations on your own by worrying. Remember that God is in control and has only your best interests at heart — no worries.

For additional copies of this book,
please contact us:

Jackie Groves
P.O. Box 68
Hudsonville, MI 49426

or visit our website:

www.danielericgroves.com

I trust this book has been a blessing to you. If you wish to use it for group study or simply for gift-giving, please inquire about quantity discounts.

Please note: the subsequent pages have been designed to enable you to Journal your own walk as you meditate on these brief devotionals.

My Thoughts

My Thoughts

My Thoughts

My Thoughts

_____

_____

_____

_____

_____

_____

_____

_____

_____

_____

_____

_____

_____

_____

_____

_____

_____

_____

My Thoughts

My Thoughts

_____

_____

_____

_____

_____

_____

_____

_____

_____

_____

_____

_____

_____

_____

_____

_____

My Thoughts

My Thoughts

My Thoughts